FIND the SLEEPER

An Untold Story

© 2020 by Dr. JK Ortiz
email: kntr@msn.com
Website: drjkortiz.com

Scripture taken from the New King James Version
Copyright © 1982 by Thomas Nelson.
Used by permission. All rights reserved.

Free photo 94250775 © Publicdomainphotos
dreamtime.com
© Creative Commons Zero (CC0)

COPYRIGHTED © 2020

FIND the SLEEPER

CONTENT

FIND the SLEEPER

DEDICATION

Thanks to my wife Adaliz, and children
Gabriel, Elijah, and Itzak for their unrelenting
support without whom this book would have
not been possible.

Thanks to my parents, Pablo and Gloria E. Ortiz, who instructed me in the way of the Lord
since childhood. Unfortunately, both passed
away before having the opportunity to see this
book come to fruition.

FIND the SLEEPER

INTRODUCTION

W hat if . . . What if you were told, that in making one single rational decision, the current storm in your life would forever disappear? Would you be convinced to act if you were provided with actions to take? Would you like to have the howling winds that are destroying your sails come to a full stop, changing the landscape of your life as you know it? Would you be willing to put into action counter measures? The violent waves smashing against your ship are erasing the likelihood of being able to safely return to port. What price would you be willing to pay to prevent irreversible losses in your life and irreparable damages to you and your family? What if you were told that the answer to remove the storm, silence the howling winds, and calm the intense waves depends on you and you alone? What would you say if you were told that the decision to be made is found within the context of the Scriptures, which have made it to these pages? It is going to require knowledge, wisdom, and most importantly courage to act in order to bring the storm into submission. How would you react if you were told that the time to make that decision is now? In the pages that lie ahead we will continue to explore the verses found in this passage of the Scripture. The story of Jonah has had such a profound message to those who seek to understand its application in their day to day living. The retelling of Jonah's story will open your mind and cause you a formidable storm of thoughts like you have never before experienced in your life. The decision to be made will not be an easy one, but it is a decision that could transform your life in the same way that it transformed mine. The message brought to you within the context of this book is more than a human interpretation of the events that unfolded on that nightmarish day of Jonah. It is a revelation from the Most High obtained during a difficult time in my life. A pulpit from which to preach or expose the story of Jonah in an elegant and eloquent manner as those before me does not exist for me. I do not have that privilege. There is neither an auditorium full of hundreds of congregants listening to my amplified voice as it is pushed through loud speakers pointed in every direction. This book is the platform afforded to me by the Lord. I must write what He teaches me. Writing is my voice, and you are my audience. Rest assure that these pages have been divinely inspired for the knowledge and understanding of the events that are occurring in your life; a life that is about to change. Therefore, open your heart to receive words that will permanently transform your life and the lives of those around you. The time has come for your storm to end. You have prayed loud enough, you have struggled hard enough, and you have waited long enough.

Chapter **1**

ARISE

Now the word of the Lord came to Jonah the son of Amittai, saying, 'Arise, go to Nineveh, that great city, and cry against it; for their wickedness is come up before me.'" Jonah 1:1-2

The biblical story of Jonah is a story that has been told and preached countless of times throughout multiple generations and will continue to be passed on to future generations in various writings, including this one. We have heard it from unknown Sunday school teachers to well-known Sunday preachers. Pastors and leaders from small city churches to big city mega-churches have presented sermons on this biblical story of epic proportion. It has been preached from the altar of churches throughout the world, and in many different languages and dialects. The story of Jonah has also been preached on street corners across the nations. It even has been talked about on the radio. Everyone has heard of the story of Jonah to some extent.

The subject of disobedience and the consequences that arise from such a blunt and purposeful act are the focus points of the teachings. Preachers and teachers place focus on the futile attempt to run and hide from a living God. However, the story of Jonah is not a story to be merely used to instill the fear of the Lord in the minds of individuals and nor should it be used only to remind worshipers of the consequences of their disobedience. It is not to be relegated only to children books either. As appealing as it is to children due to the presence of a sea creature in the story that swallows a whole man, Jonah's story is not to be solely used as a numbered coloring book, assisting the child artist, if you will, in completing the task for a predetermined outcome, where one has to stay within the lines in order for the finished drawing to have an aesthetically pleasing look.

The story of Jonah is a story that begs a soul-searching voyage into our own deep and sometimes obscured heart, completely in line with the Scriptures' teaching that one must look inward into our own self before looking outward (Matthew 7:3). But who wants to look into the depths of their own soul, searching for whatever evil or darkness might exist or lurk within? For the most part, Jonah's teachings are often limited to the punishment associated with an act of disobedience. No more. As difficult as it may be, self evaluation must be done during any given storm to minimize its negative effect on the lives of those around us.

In verse one, we can clearly see that a mandate was given to Jonah. It clearly specifies who, where, what, and why. Within this verse alone we learn that the Lord's instructions are precise and clear. First, the part of who told who is answered, "... the Lord." The Lord told Jonah. It was not something that Jonah concocted or schemed himself. He was not being led by his own flesh or desire to become a prophet. Clearly, Jonah was not looking to become the prime example of what not to do when the Word of the Lord comes unto us. Who strives to be the picture next to the definition of disobedience in a dictionary, or the Holy Scriptures? Surely, being included in the best and most printed and translated book in the history of mankind was not his intent either, as it was not being compiled at the time. The Lord instructing Jonah reminds us that it is He that instructs, it is He who leads us, it is He who is in control, and not the other way around. Yet, there are those walking among the living today that act and pray as if they tell the Lord what to do. Care must be taken when prayers are solemnly uttered from our lips. Just because the Word of God says ask and you shall receive and knock and it will be answered unto you (Matthew 7:7) it does not give anyone the authority to usurp the throne of the Most High or the authority to instruct God on what He should do and how He should do it under the disguise of a solemn prayer. If there is something that the Lord himself does not share, it is his Glory (Isaiah 42:8). Let us keep in mind the spiritual chain of command when elevating our prayers unto Him.

Second, the part of where is also answered. The Lord told Jonah to go to Nineveh, the great city. The message that is to be delivered is not for any other city other than Nineveh. As we already know, Jonah was not thrilled to warn Nineveh of the impending destruction of the city and its people. Jonah was asked to go to people whom he did not like or empathized. They were not like him. Therefore, the message is specific as to who and where. Many times the message to be delivered is intended to people we do not necessarily agree with. Yet, it must be delivered.

Third, the what is answered. Jonah was instructed by the Lord to go to Nineveh to do something. It was not to visit his relatives, if he had any there, or to get away from it all. He was asked to go to sin city and cry out against it. The message from the Lord to be cried out was clear in that respect. Why? Because Nineveh's wickedness had come before the Lord. In other words, their acts were evil.

Moses knew where he was going. The reason that the Israelites wandered for approximately 40 years in the desert was due to their disobedience and rebellious ways, but Moses knew the destination. Abraham knew where he was going despite that he sojourned the land and his descendants possessed the Promised Land more than 400 years later. The Lord had told him he was going to a distant land that had been given to him and his ancestors as inheritance. The elected Church also knows where it is going. We are just waiting patiently for His triumphant return. When the Word of the Lord comes to you, it lets you know where you are going; specifics come later. All that is required is an act of obedience, because obedience is greater than sacrifice (1 Samuel 15:22).

If the assignment given to you does not answer all proposed pertinent questions as to who, what, where, and why, or if there is no clarity as to who, what, where, and why, sit still until all questions are clearly identified, answered, and understood or the mission might fail.

Do you have a calling from the Lord to go somewhere or a Word to deliver to someone that has not been delivered yet in a deliberate act of disobedience? Is there a current storm in your life, clouds hovering above and winds causing your ship to be tossed around in the waves? Are the winds of a storm tearing up your sails, changing your direction, causing you to spend more energy attempting to re-direct your ship to its intended destination?

If the story of Jonah sounds too familiar and you find yourself in the same position as Jonah, with a command to deliver a message to someone, do not procrastinate, deliver the message without hesitation as the Lord commanded you and move on. In doing so, the storm will cease and you will not find yourself in the same predicament as Jonah.

However, if you are not trying to flee from the Lord, give praises unto the Living God. Rejoice and dance! Yet, continue exploring the content of these pages, as you will someday be able to deliver someone from a storm in his or her life with the knowledge obtained herein. Perhaps the revelation found in this book will allow you to someday con-quer, or more importantly, avoid a future storm in

your life as you constantly arise in the right direction at the command of the Lord's voice.

Find the Sleeper

Chapter **2**

TRIP TO TARSHISH

But Jonah arose to flee to Tarshish from the presence of the Lord. He went down to Joppa, and he found a ship going to Tarshish; so he paid the fare, and went down into it, to go with them to Tarshish from the presence of the Lord."
Jonah 1:3

J onah heard the clear and precise call and acted on it. However, his intent to not obey was purposely clear and meticulously planned. He was not at any cost going to pay the citizens of Nineveh a visit to deliver the message that was given unto him. His mind was set. Rather, Jonah rose and fled to Tarshish. He was determined to do exactly the opposite of the Word that was given to him by the Lord. He casually travelled down to Joppa and found a ship. Finding a ship implies some level of difficulty in his search for a ship that would allow him to board, but Jonah was determined. One can only speculate the quantity of ships that refused to take Jonah onboard as a passenger. Jonah may have attempted to board a ship at three or four other port locations on his way down to Joppa, heading away from the presence of the Lord. As difficult as God was making it for him to disobey, Jonah was equally persistent until a ship was eventually found and the asking price was paid, clearly sending the Lord a message of who Jonah thought was in control.

Being able to obtain a ticket to anywhere at the last minute at a reasonable price is nearly an impossible feat to accomplish. All seats or tickets to a special event are usually sold out if one waits for the last minute. If there is any availability, the price for the ticket is an exorbitant amount. One can safely assume that booking a trip is no different today than it was back in the days of Jonah. The cost of the trip to Tarshish must have been a substantial and staggering amount.

Can you imagine the cost of obtaining a last minute flight to any city in the world when one is in a hurry? Likewise for Jonah, it must have been difficult to find a willing vessel to take him on board. The negotiations for a reasonable price must have been intense. Yet, regardless of cost and class, Jonah paid the fare, and went down into the ship en route to Tarshish. However, it was not the people of Tarshish that needed to hear the message given to Jonah. It was not the city of Tarshish that Jonah needed to cry against. Yet, here is Jonah, inside the ship of a newly found friend, heading to Tarshish, fleeing from the presence of the Lord at any cost, to possibly proclaim a message of destruction that was meant for someone else.

We are not sure what was going through Jonah's mind and we will never find out. However, one can speculate that in Jonah's heart the people of Tarshish were more worthy of a message than the people of Nineveh. Who knows, perhaps God already had sent a prophet to speak to the people of Tarshish and had determined to send Jonah to Nineveh instead. Maybe Tarshish was going to be Jonah's next destination. Nobody knows. What we know is that when the Lord sends, we must obey or we risk seeing the formation of a storm and the devastation that comes with it if we do not change our mindset.

After the calling, the actions that immediately follow determine the environment that will eventually surround you. The environment does not define you, yet with time, the environment becomes part of the landscape, making it seem like the norm. Jonah opted to ignore the Lord and decided to flee from His presence and the landscape of a storm became his norm. Though the storm may have been for a brief moment, it must have felt like an eternity. When the Word of the Lord comes, it must be obeyed and not ignored. One must remember the who, the what, the where, and the why of the message. There is no way around it. Your decision will determine what sort of winds will propel your ship. The winds subtlety or its violent nature depends on the actions taken, the disposition of the heart, and our willingness to obey.

Did you arise to go in the opposite direction from where you were told to go that could explain the storm in your life? Have you been attempting to redirect your ship because the winds are blowing you off course? If so, what types of efforts were made to flee from the presence of the Lord? The longer the storm persists over you, the more drastic maneuvers at sea must be taken to change direction and safely return to port, if it is even possible.

Maybe you are not fleeing from the Lord but rather ignoring the voice of the Lord. Have you thought about examining your past? Perhaps some time ago a call was made to you that you no longer remember. Perhaps there is a lingering promise that needs to be made whole. Keep in mind that it is better not to promise than to promise and not fulfill (Ecclesiastes 5:5).

Being able to answer these proposed questions is a great start to determine if one is in the same historical path of destruction that Jonah traveled. In order for the storm to dissipate and for the winds to stop, we must retrace our steps and profoundly examine our past decisions. In doing so, we can then determine the reason for the storm and what fuels it. It is not easy to look into our own hearts and examine it against His heart. I know, it is a scary feeling; however, it is part of the process and it must be done. Examining our hearts against His should be undertaken daily.

By now, I hope that you have searched deep within yourself for a reason that could explain the presence of the storm in your life. However, you find that there is no reason for the howling winds that push you in every direction, and that the waves that crash against, around, and about the ship are an unexplained phenomenon. The decisions you have made have been sound. No divine callings in the past have been ignored. No promises have been unkept. Definitely you are not fleeing at all from anything or anyone, including the Lord. No one is chasing you. Yet, there is a storm over your life and it is real.

The words that follow will continue to open your heart and soul for that decision that will have to eventually take place. The answer to calming your storm, quieting the winds, and taking command of the waves is only a few pages away. Do not stop your quest for your answer here, rather remain faithful in your reading. As the farmer plows the land before the seed is planted, your heart is being prepared to receive what will be asked of you to do. Hopefully, you will not entertain the thought of fleeing from the presence of the Lord like Jonah did.

Chapter **3**

THE GREAT WIND

"But the Lord sent out a great wind on the sea, and there was a mighty tempest on the sea, so that the ship was about to be broken up ." Jonah 1:4

The Lord requested Jonah to go on a journey to cry against a city whose wickedness had reached the presence of the Lord. Jonah was asked to deliver a message of destruction as impending doom was looming over the city. However, Jonah decided to take matters into his own hands and decided to be the judge, jury, and executioner. Mercy should not be afforded to such

29

wicked people according to Jonah's law. The city must be destroyed and demolished with all its citizens driven to nonexistence. It never entered Jonah's mind or heart that there could be, and there were, children in the city, newborns and infants alike. He was not interested in God having mercy on the wicked people of Nineveh. Unlike Abraham who negotiated with God prior to the destruction of Sodom and Gomorrah (Genesis 18:16-33), Jonah was nonchalant in seeking the destruction of Nineveh. It did not matter to Jonah if there was one or one hundred citizens in Nineveh that were righteous. He was neither interested in asking nor learning. Perhaps that is the reason why Abraham was called a friend of God (James 2:23), and Jonah . . . well, Jonah is Jonah.

The destruction of Nineveh could not have come at a better time for Jonah. In doing so, neglecting to carry the message, unbeknown to him, Jonah's actions were attempting to unseat God from his throne and relegate God to be Jonah's law enforcer, as determine by Jonah's code of justice. God was not pleased with it as he does not share His Glory with anyone. I mean no one. As I understand it, the last one that tried to sit on God's throne ended up being thrown out of Heaven with all his followers. Therefore, as a result of Jonah's blunt disobedience, the Lord sent a great wind on the sea. Notice here that only a great wind was sent. The Lord did not send the storm, nor did He send the waves. The Lord did not ask the sea to open up and expose its terrifying depths with a massive display of overarching waves that pounded the ship left to right, from above and below, almost into oblivion. It was just a great wind. However, the longer the great winds persisted the worse the situation became for Jonah as the storm formed and intensified. Remember, the winds fuel the storm. The formation of the tempest or storm, and the waves that crashed about and against the boat were the result of intensified winds. The storm and the waves were part of a cascading event; a result of the great winds sent by the Lord. Therefore, if the winds dissipate, the storm disappears.

There was no intent from the Lord to tear the ship apart and send it to the oceans's ship graveyard. The storm that eventually formed tossed the ship about like a paper boat. The ship was about to be broken up. Key phrase here is "about to be broken up." The Lord's intent was likely to redirect the ship back to its port of origin and not to destroy it, affording Jonah another opportunity to make the right decision. However, the captain and mariners reached a point of no return. Jonah needed to go back to Joppa, disembark, and head back to Nineveh where he was sent.

If destruction was needed to accomplish the Lord's objective, then destruction of the ship would have occurred. Persistent disobedience leads to destruction, a last ditch effort that leads to long lasting changes. It is interesting that the same man who did not want the Lord to show mercy towards the great city of Nineveh was now enjoying the mercy of the Living God as he was being kept alive inside a vessel at sea.

Is there a storm in your life as a result of a wrong turn or a personal objective that goes against what you have been asked to do by the Lord? Have you ever without realizing it cast judgment upon someone just because you disagreed with them, or because they did something to you that was unforgivable, hoping the worst comes upon them? Are the winds persistently blowing you away from your intended destination? Remember, if the winds persist a storm will form. The longer a storm hovers over your life the more likely that it will lead to crashing waves and a ship or life that appears to be breaking or as the verse says "about to be broken up" (Jonah 1:4). The purpose of the winds is not to destroy you, but rather for you to reassess your situation and make necessary adjustments, leading you back in the right direction, before reaching that point of no return.

Remember that when God sends the winds, the winds arrive at the command of His voice. His word never comes back empty, rather it goes and accomplishes that for which it was sent and returns to Him (Isaiah 55:11). In other words, the storm over your life will not cease to exist until the winds are called back and its purpose fulfilled. So, why fight it? Why challenge the Almighty?

Hopefully by now you are beginning to feel the winds, see the waves, and notice the storm in your life. Hopefully it is all becoming clear. It is in this disposition of acceptance when changes happen, wisdom emerges, and courage takes form, leading to action. The storm in your life may have nothing to do with disobedience as in the case of Jonah. The storm in your life may have nothing to do with expecting someone to be punished for their actions or your disobedience. It is not a case of you not showing mercy. However, there is no denying that the storm in your life is all about you. The question that remains unanswered is what action or inaction was taken to cause the Lord to send a great wind into your life. Have you subconsciously become the judge, jury, and executioner? I respectfully do not think so.

Find the Sleeper

Chapter **4**

FAST ASLEEP

Then the mariners were afraid; and every man
cried out to his god, and threw the cargo that was
in the ship into the sea, to lighten the load. But
Jonah had gone down into the lowest parts of the
ship, had lain down, and was fast asleep."
Jonah 1:5

Without a doubt, a storm will cause everyone to seek shelter and to engage in protective actions and defensive maneuvers in order to keep safe their most valuable possessions, including their loved ones. Because of hurricane winds, windows are boarded up with any kind of material available at hand. Flood insurance is commonly purchased in low level areas to cover for losses as a result of rising waters. With every hurricane threatening to make landfall, people rush to building supply stores in search of must have items to assist during expected long periods of electrical blackouts or food shortages, leaving store shelves empty as if the end of the world was near. A storm produces rational and irrational fears in the lives of those in its path.

In the midst of a storm with howling winds and crashing waves, fear will definitely set in and make itself home in the mind and heart of any individual. It does need to be invited in and certainly, it is never welcomed. However, fear is a normal human reaction experienced by everyone at some point in their life, as the human instinct autonomically transitions into survival mode. Have you been on a plane flight where the plane is flying through an electrical storm? Lightning and rain abounds.

The ups and downs, the left and right banking dives in an attempt to find a path of least resistance can be quite uncomfortable and scary. During certain flights, breathing masks will even drop from above due to the sudden loss of cabin pressure. Panic and chaos ensues. Screams can sometimes be heard. It is a situation where passengers begin to examine their spiritual life, causing them to send prayers to their gods for protection and forgiveness with supplications that are silently spoken from their hearts and minds. The pride within self or the fear of offending the listener will not allow them to speak them audibly.

Due to Jonah's act of disobedience, a great wind was sent and it evolved into a storm of epic proportions. When the storm reached the boiling point, thoughts became irrational and reasoning got out of control. Naturally the mariners experienced most profound fear and as a result they began to pray and cry unto their gods. These mariners were not novice mariners. It was not their first rodeo. These mariners knew what they were against and what needed to be done in order to save the ship, the lives of those aboard the ship, and, most importantly, their lives. When every skillful defensive maneuver at their disposal failed, they began to throw their cargo into the sea to lighten the load, allowing the ship to be easily maneuvered in the violent and dark waters that surrounded it. The lighter ship made it easier for the ship to stay above the waters, preventing it from easily sinking into a dismal abyss, taking their lives with it.

Jonah, on the other hand, having gone down into the lower parts of the ship had fallen fast asleep. He had made himself comfortable in the middle of the storm; too comfortable if you were to ask me. Someone once said that actions speak louder than words. Jonah's demeanor and attitude towards the people of Nineveh is unquestionably demonstrated by his actions. His actions spoke louder and louder with every passing moment. Not only did he not have any desire for the Lord to show mercy towards the people of Nineveh but also no concern for the life of the mariners, not even his own. So he slept soundly. Jonah had entered a depressive state that made him dangerous and toxic to anyone around him. According to Jonah, the mariners at sea were just as bad as the people of Nineveh for they served false gods. The stance that Jonah had taken was that everyone must perish, and he was not a bit remorseful. He was either going to live by it or die by it.

Sadly, there are Christians in these times that exhibit toward others the same attitude that Jonah exhibited toward the citizens of Nineveh and the mariners at sea. The compassion and mercy afforded to them by the Lord does not appear to extend to anyone else. We are quick to cast stones and murmur about the rise and fall of fellow worshipers, including Pastors, forgetting that they too endure the same trials, temptations, and tribulations that we all face. Just because others worship differently, dress differently, or speak differently, judgement is cast upon them by some, forgetting that the Lord left written in the Scriptures that He does not want anyone to perish but have everlasting life (John 3:16), and that we must first remove the plank in our eyes before pointing to the speck in someone else's eye (Luke 6:42).

Our act of disobedience or selfish behavior, one that mimics Jonah's, can cause people that are observing us closely to pray, worship, and cry to their false gods just like the mariners at sea. Have you ever thought that instead of drawing people closer to the one and only Living God your actions and words may be having a paradoxical effect, driving them far away from Him? That is not how I want to be remembered living this life, and, in all honesty, neither should you be remembered that way. I would not want to be responsible for causing anyone to worship false gods.

As Christians, we need to be obedient to the Word of God when it comes. The act of fleeing from the Lord should not even come to mind when asked by the Lord to deliver a word of affirmation or warning. Unfortunately, there are many who not only attempt to flee from the Lord but also sleep through their storm as if there were no consequences to their destructive behavior, ignoring their call. They are willing and ready to go down with the ship at any cost just like Jonah, taking down with them anyone in their path. Nothing matters to them as long as they get their way.

Have you been sleeping through the winds of your storm? Are you impervious to the howling winds and crashing waves that pound the stern of the ship? Have you stopped caring about others safety? Have you considered how your actions are affecting everyone else around you? If any of these proposed questions do not describe your current spiritual condition or state of being, you must continue to search for the answer that will calm the storm in your life, dissipate the winds, and calm the waters. In doing so, you will be able to return to shore where you belong, provided you have not reached a point of no return. You will be able to retrace your steps, returning to a path of obedience, and perhaps most importantly, obtain blessings for you and your family.

You are certain and convinced that you are not fleeing from the Lord and that you are not in an act of disobedience. You are definitely not sleeping through your storm. Yet, your life continues to be battered by a storm. You are barely surviving the storm irrespective of the howling winds battering the sails and the crashing waves smashing against the hull. You cannot take it anymore. You have reached a point where you are willing to do anything to make the storm history, a thing of the past.

Speaking to it does not work. Praying has not worked. Fasting does not work either. Good works has not helped you. You are afraid and for a good reason.

It is at this breaking point in your life where God really wants you, being receptive to His word and in a state of desperate disposition to obey. This desperate stage in our lives is where all of our human efforts have been attempted and exhausted. It is when we have done all we know to do and can do and still have failed. Even those things learned from countless Sunday-preached sermons do not provide any resolve. Everything has failed. Why? Because the Lord does not share His glory with anyone, and the Glory will be all His when the storm dissipates. Even if the answer is revealed to you by the message read within this manuscript, the glory will always be His.

Find the Sleeper

Chapter **5**

THE CAPTAIN

"So the captain came to him and said to him, 'What do you mean sleeper? Arise, call on your God; perhaps your God will consider us, so that we may not perish.'" Jonah 1:6

L et us briefly recap. After receiving the word from the Lord, we have seen how Jonah had a predetermined purpose in his own heart to defy the command from the Lord. He rose as instructed but not to travel to Nineveh. Rather, Jonah rose to flee from the presence of the Lord. Ending up in Joppa after not being able to find a ship to board in several other previous ports, Jonah paid an exorbitant price for his ticket out of town. He boards the ship and heads straight down to the lowest parts of the ship. And if that was not all, he falls asleep. He was going to Tarshish and there was nothing the Lord could do about it, or so he thought. Then we see how the Lord sends out a great wind on the sea, leading to a mighty tempest. The waves like a domino effect followed, tossing the ship like it was about to break. Fear of death possesses the mariners at sea, causing each and everyone to start crying out and praying to their gods.

When everything fails, a consensus is reached and a plan is implemented. They decided to toss overboard their cargo in order to lighten the load in an attempt to lighten the ship and make it more maneuverable so that they could at least bring it back to port. However, that too failed. Which brings us to verse six in the first chapter of the book of Jonah.

Nothing worked and they had run out of ideas and possible solutions. When all efforts failed, the captain realized that there was something strange about this storm. He had seen storms before and had managed to survive previous storms. The storm that was assailing them was foreign to the captain, unusual at best. The captain, probably worried about his crew and passengers, took a head count and realized that Jonah was missing. Realizing that no one saw Jonah helping toss anything overboard he decided to investigate. Thinking perhaps Jonah was lost at sea, a whole wide ship search for him ensued. However, the captain found him sleeping in the lowest part of the ship. This did not bode well with the captain who then commands Jonah to "Arise."

Jonah had heard the word arise before, when the Lord had also commanded him to arise. One cannot imagine Jonah's heartbeat racing as soon as the word arise was spoken from the captain's lips. His heart must have been pounding, his thoughts racing, adrenaline rushing, realizing the Lord had found him yet again. Prophet Jonah must have forgotten that no one can hide from the presence of the Lord; something King David and Jeremiah knew and had already discovered (Psalms 139:7-12, Jeremiah 23:24).

The captain of the ship asked Jonah to call on his God as perhaps Jonah's God would consider their plight and deliver them from the storm so that they would not perish. Up to this moment, the captain does not know who Jonah's God is. Yet, he practically begs him to pray as their lives are in peril. The cargo is lost at sea, the ship is about to be broken up, and now their lives are on the balance. Innocent bystanders of Jonah's disobedience are about to face the wrath of the Living God. However, prayer was the last thing on Jonah's mind. As far as Jonah is concerned, he is not in speaking terms with the Lord because the Lord had the nerve to ask him to warn the people of Nineveh of their impending destruction. In fact, Jonah's attitude is that of a stubborn prophet who will only speak words from the Lord as long as he agrees with it, making himself equal to God.

Hopefully, Jonah's attitude is not your own. As Christians, we need to be obedient to the Lord despite of the circumstances or the message. We are not asked to agree with the message, we need to be obedient and deliver the message as it was given, without adding or subtracting from it. But Lord, they don't look like me! So what! But Lord they don't dress like me! Who cares! But Lord, they have a different culture! No one asked; who paid the ultimate price? But Lord, but Lord, but Lord, but Lord. Enough excuses already! Moses tried justifying not going down to Egypt and presenting himself before the Pharaoh to request the freedom and deliverance of the people of Israel. His difficulty with speech was a good reason, but not good enough to excuse him from his calling. Aaron his brother was appointed as spokesperson (Exodus 4:10-14). If Moses could not get himself excused, there was no way that Jonah was going to get away with it either. The Lord is a righteous God. Even Jesus thought that maybe there was a possible way out while praying in the garden; second thoughts rushing through his mind. He too surrendered to the will of his Father, allowing his Father's will to be done over His (Matthew 26:36-46).

If nothing of this resonates with you and there is no clarity as to the reason of the storm in your life yet, it is simply because there is no reason for the storm to be smashing you against the waves of the sea and there is no reason for the winds to toss your ship, your life, around and about, causing it to about break.

You have fasted. You have prayed. You have searched and studied the Scriptures, looking for answers. You have asked the church leaders to keep you in their prayers. Friends and family may also be praying for and over you. Counseling provided by professionals in their field of expertise has not worked. Yet, somehow, the storm remains over you. If you move, it moves with you. If you stop, it stops over you. It is like a curse, a dark shadow that follows you everywhere you go. But why?

Many books have been written attempting to answer the old age question of "Why me?"   The Holy Scriptures tells us that a servant is no greater than his master. Jesus suffered and endured false accusations, including the unrelenting punishment, that lead to his sacrifice on the cross. If they did these things unto Him, they will also do it unto us (John 15:18-25). In other words, we are not exempt of storms in our lives. Nonetheless, you argue that you have searched your heart and have found yourself to be blameless by your own standards. You are A-Ok. Then, glory be to God. You are about to soon discover the truth that was revealed to me as I endured a storm in my life. Perhaps the same struggle as you. My decision forced the winds to dissipate, causing the storm to collapse all on its own, calming the waves, providing a smooth sailing, allowing me to continue on my journey, or better yet, return to port to embark on a new journey.

This writing is not just the result of pure revelation, but the result of a revelation combined with an act of obedience. I lived this. I experienced this. I had turned to asking others in my close circle to have me in their thoughts and prayers. Perhaps the Lord would hear their prayers, the storm would dissipate, and a new dawn would ensue. The storm remained over me and it was not because my prayers and their prayers did not reach the throne of God. God heard the prayers alright. However, it was not only time for me to pray but also time for me to take action.

The written message in this book is an honest attempt to have you scrutinize your spiritual life and past decisions made. It is best to place ourselves in the balance and see where we are short and correct it rather than to have the Lord place us in His balance and find us lacking (Daniel 5:13-29). If your spiritual career path has similarities to that of Jonah's, it is highly encouraged that you seek forgiveness from the Lord and return to a spiritual disposition better than the one you were at the time the word of the Lord came to you, and reset. If your spiritual career path is nothing like that of Jonah, it is highly encouraged as well that you pray and prepare yourself for what the next step will be in your life. Of course, this only applies to those who are tired and exhausted from the storm and are willing to do something about it; mainly those in a desperate disposition to obey.

If you like your storm, you can definitely keep it. You should not be pressured to do anything you do not want to do. It is your decision to make. Just keep in mind that the longer the storm remains over you and the longer you remain inactive, the storm will become the norm in your life and great will be your loss.

Chapter **6**

FOUND AGAIN

"They said to one another, 'Come, let us cast lots, that we may know for whose cause this trouble has come upon us.' So they cast lots, and the lot fell on Jonah." Jonah 1:7

Bringing down the sails of the ship, praying to their gods, and throwing overboard the cargo found on the ship had no impact on the storm. The storm heavily intensified with no end in sight. One can safely assume that lighting became more prominent, the water swells intensified, and the waves grew bigger in stature. Water is all over the deck, the stern, and the bow. The mast is possibly broken and the sails, if any left, broken, flapping with the winds. Fear, chaos, and confusion is everywhere. Everyone begins to blame everyone like little children fighting in the school yard. Soaked and wet from the ocean's water, tired of fighting a relentless storm that refuses to subside, with the taste of sea salt in their mouths, the mariners continue to quarrel, attempting to find a solution that pleased everyone on board the ship, searching for a solution that would bring them home safely. Eventually, the mariners reach an agreement.

One cannot imagine the conversations that took place in the midst of such a chaotic environment where fear abounded. They reached a consensus to cast lots and find out what and who is the cause and root of the problem. At this point they believe that this is a divine storm sent by a god due to someone's misbehavior or, should we say, disobedience. The storm is getting stronger, which supports their suspicion of divine involvement, emboldening their desire to act.

Casting lots is an ancient way of resolving disputes. When two or more individuals could not arrive to an amicable resolution beneficial to all parties involved, casting lots would settle the dispute. The end result of such action would be accepted as divine intervention, regardless of how unfair or impartial the outcome may be seemed by any participant. In the midst of all this confusion and arguments, Jonah remained calm, not a word spoken. They were still probably waiting for him to pray. He was so mad at the Lord for asking him to warn Nineveh that he did not even pray when asked by the captain. A simple prayer would have sufficed. So they cast lots. The methodical approach or systematic deliverance of casting lots is inconsequential to the outcome. Truth is what matters, and that truth is that the lot fell on Jonah and Jonah was found once again.

Someone once said that silence is golden. However, there are times when we must speak as Christians and let our voice be heard, a profound message found in the book of Esther. The destruction of the people of Israel would have had an easy road to success had it not been for Queen Esther who boldly presented her case before the King, after being counseled by her cousin (Esther 4:16). Like Esther, who declared who she truly was to the King, Jonah could have volunteered his plight, his act of disobedience, to the captain and fellow mariners. A prayer of repentance by Jonah would have possibly ensued and all would have been well. Well, not all, since they had already thrown the cargo overboard. But Jonah chose to remain silent. Not only did Jonah's act of disobedience cause the mariners to pray and get closer to their false gods, but also his silence led them to seek answers in the most unusual place, luck. Jonah knew that the storm in which they found themselves was because of him. He was pleased and content with it. He had come to terms with it. The destruction of Nineveh would fall on his shoulders and he was willing to live with it, or die.

You do not have to be content with your storm. Do not settle in and make yourself comfortable. All that is needed is an act of repentance. A prayer of forgiveness will do if you find that you are in disobedience to the word of God. Once that prayer reaches the throne of the Living God, the winds will subside and with it the storm.

But you are tired of sending prayers into the heavens with no answer in return. The storm is still there, remaining in sight, strong and bold. You can taste the salty water and visibility at this point is nearly zero nautical miles. Visible and palpable, the storm continues its path of destruction. Yet, there is no solution in sight, You may even be tempted to consider casting lots of some sort. Be careful and do not fall victim by looking for answers in the occult.

Church going people visiting palm and card readers, reading daily horoscopes, under the pretense that it is for entertainment only is sadly becoming an accepted practice simply because we have remained silent. Let me inform you that you must remain faithful during this trajectory of unforeseen delay or silence from the Lord. God's silence or presumptive delay should be more convincing proof and reason that we ought to stand still and know that He is God (Psalms 46:10). Saul sought to seek answers from the witch of Endor, a medium (1st Samuel 28:7-25), when he could not find the answer he sought from prophets in the land, costing him the kingdom and his life. Do not commit the same act of desperation. The answer you seek is about to be revealed and the storm is about to subside if the prescribed measures are taken. Believe me. It subsided for me.

For the past few years you have been begging for a resolution to your storm. No matter what you do, blessings do not fall on you, yet, they fall on others. They prosper and advance in their career. They have a prosperous and peaceful life. Their family is well. In no circumstances you are coveting because that would be breaking a commandment (Exodus 20:17). You are just wondering why is it that you cannot move forward. You are questioning why are you stuck in a vicious cycle if you are doing the same thing as your fellow man. You cannot advance. The wheels are spinning but you are stuck. There is no forward motion. All efforts lead nowhere. You are being tossed about and around by the winds.

The port is within your sight, yet, you cannot reach it. Your ship is still at sea with you in it, battling a storm and losing precious cargo. If only you could make the storm disappear, all would be well. If only the Lord would hear your prayer. Well . . . I have good news for you. He has. His silence is broken through this revelation.

Chapter **7**

QUESTIONS

"Then they said to him, 'Please tell us! For whose cause is this trouble upon us? What is your occupation? And where do you come from? What is your country? And of what people are you?'"
Jonah 1:8

Things are beginning to heat up on the ship, questions are being asked and answers must be provided. Everybody except Jonah has stated their story and has had to answer a routine questionnaire, likely developed after a consensus was reached. The answers provided by everyone on the ship were not found to have any correlation or interconnection with the storm. There was no smoking gun; probably another reason why they went looking for Jonah.

Jonah got away with not praying. Maybe he thought he would get away with it once again. But the lot fell on Jonah and it was time he revealed his condition. It was story time. It was time for him to answer the pertinent questions presented before him and complete the survey. His silence was going to be broken at last. The mariners at sea had suffered enough and time had run out. They reached a point of no return, finding themselves in a desperate disposition to obey.

Up to this point, even though the lot fell on Jonah, the mariners did not know the reason for the storm. They only knew that the lot fell on Jonah. So naturally they begin to ask Jonah questions in an attempt to get clarification from him. At this point, they only knew that Jonah had the answer to their problem.

Can you imagine the tension on the ship? The silence that erupted left everyone speechless. The screams stopped. The prayers ceased. Fear existed no longer. All eyes were fixated on Jonah, a staring contest of some sort. The mariners did not care any longer about the storm, the waves, or the winds, or even the ship. The cargo was already tossed overboard and floating at sea, a constant reminder of what they had lost. There was nothing to worry about but their lives at this point. Everything around them appears to be still, frozen in time, a picture to remember. They are focused, trying to determine what exactly is occurring around them. With all of their combined skills and maritime expertise they were not able to manage getting out of the storm. They are hunting for answers and their sights are squared on Jonah. Yet, the captain and mariners maintain their composure and proceed to ask Jonah; "Please tell us! For whose cause is this trouble upon us? What is your occupation? And where do you come from? What is your country? And of what people are you?" (Jonah 1:8).

Suddenly, Jonah's silence was broken when he stated, "I am a Hebrew; and I fear the Lord, the God of heaven, who made the sea and the dry land" (Jonah 1:9) and went on to say that he was fleeing from the presence of the Lord.

I would have loved to see the expression on the faces of the mariners when Jonah said that he feared the Lord. Really Jonah, you fear the Lord? You, the prophet, a Hebrew, fleeing from His presence, fear the Lord? It is fascinating how many Christians claim to fear the Lord today and continue to run a race against time, pretending to be obedient to the word of God, yet, fleeing from him, not accepting the calling from the Lord, denying themselves and those around them of His abundance of mercy and grace.

In those times, being a Hebrew said a lot about the person's background. Not only did Jonah say that he was a Hebrew but also that he was a servant of the Most High God. The mariners immediately recognized the trouble that had befallen on them. They were dealing with someone who worshiped the God of Israel. The wonders and marvels that God had done to free the Israelites from Egypt had already been spread throughout the land many years before. They were "exceedingly afraid, and said to him, 'Why have you done this?'" (Jonah 1:10).

At first, they were afraid due to the storm. Now they are exceedingly afraid due to the predicament in which they found themselves, thanks to Jonah. Forget the storm. They have a Hebrew prophet on board who has upset the One and Only God: The God who split the Red Sea (Exodus 14), the Jordan River (Joshua 3), and the God who brought down the walls of Jericho (Joshua 6).

They had a Hebrew on board who had challenged the God who destroyed the inhabitants of Canaan and gave the land to His people. The same God was challenged by the Pharaoh of Egypt to no avail as He brought upon them plague after plague. Jonah was unlike any other passenger before him. You cannot blame the mariners for being exceedingly afraid. I would have been very afraid too, and so should you.

Chapter **8**

ANSWERS

"Then they said to him, 'What shall we do to you that the sea may be calm for us?' And he said to them, 'Pick me up and throw me into the sea; then the sea will become calm for you. For I know that this great tempest is because of me.'"
Jonah 1:11-12

This brings us to the question that we all have been wanting someone to answer: What do I need to do? The question for which you have faithfully continued reading and have patiently awaited was previously proposed by the mariners and the captain of the ship heading to

Tarshish as stated in the book of Jonah. The Scripture also tells us that there is nothing new under the sun (Ecclesiastes 1:9). Nothing. You are not and have not been the only one with a storm over his or her life asking this same question. You will not be the last one either. Trust me on that. The only difference is that you have been asking God, instead of a man or a prophet, what it is that you need to do for the storm to be calmed for you.

As the mariners asked Jonah the question, "what shall we do to you that the sea may be calm for us?" the storm continued to intensify. God was waiting for no one. His purpose would be fulfilled. Time was running out. The mariners had figured out the reason for the storm. Previously they had discovered that Jonah was to blame for it. Now they will learn what needs to be done to bring the storm into submission. While Jonah wanted to play a strong hand, the Lord matched his hand and raised him a storm. The storm became more tempestuous.

If the winds were strong before, rest assure that the winds doubled in speed and strength, leading to larger waves. Darkness surrounded the ship and the lives of those on board, including Jonah. The situation became so dire that Jonah instructs them, essentially, to treat him like cargo and to toss him overboard. In doing so, not only would the storm end the mariners' misery but also Jonah's misery as well. Jonah could have asked for other methods of resolution. But he would rather die than warn the people of the great city of Nineveh of their destruction.

The mariners knew that the fate of Jonah was already destined, reason for which they said "that the sea may be calmed for US." Jonah also knew his fate was already determined as he stated that "the sea will become calmed for YOU." Regardless of the outcome, both Jonah and the mariners knew that the storm would not cease for Jonah. Both knew that their lives had been affected forever with their encounter. Darkness shining in the middle of a stormy night.

Interestingly enough, even after learning who Jonah was and what he was up to, the mariners felt compassion for the life of Jonah. It is interesting to note that Jonah had not taken into consideration the lives of the mariners when he boarded the ship to Tarshish, fleeing from God. Yet, here we have a group of mariners who worship and pray to false gods showing more mercy and grace to Jonah than what Jonah offered them, even after finding out that it was because of Jonah that they lost all of their cargo and almost perished. They could have just tossed him overboard without hesitation. Yet, in all honesty, they attempted to row hard to return the ship to land, attempting to avoid the inevitable, homicide. However, their attempt was futile as the tempest grew stronger.

The realization that there was only one solution to the situation at hand was a heavy one. The mariners were about to murder someone. Can you imagine the pain and agony felt in the hearts and minds of those about to toss Jonah into the tempestuous waters, knowing full well that the probability of survival in those treacherous waves was absolutely zero? The tears in the eyes of those carrying out the orders must have been flowing like a cascade, discernible from the storm rain. Perhaps they cast lots again to choose those who would directly participate in the historical event. The sobbing could have been heard over the howling winds and thundering clouds. Blood was about to be on their hands. It was not an easy choice and one that was not taken lightly. A consensus was likely reached again. Instead of praying to their gods, the mariners this time turned to the God of Jonah, the Hebrew prophet, and cried to the Lord, "'We pray O Lord, please do not let us perish for this man's life, and do not charge us with innocent blood; for you, O Lord, have done as it pleased you.' So they picked up

Jonah and threw him into the sea and the sea ceased from its raging." (Jonah 1:14).

Whatever happened on that ship changed the lives of those mariners forever. The tossing and turning that must have followed the sleepless and nightmarish nights would have led some, if not all of them, to long-lasting emotional damage. Retrospectively, my prayers are with them, and presently, my prayers are with you as you will soon learn.

Chapter **9**

OVERBOARD

*"So they picked up Jonah and threw him into the
sea, and the sea ceased from its raging."*
Jonah 1:15

You have arrived to the conclusion of a
story that includes laughter, joy, misery,
and anguish. Laughter and joy because
some of the mariners and passengers in that ship
were possibly returning home to their loved ones
from a hard day of work at sea. They had no idea
what was about to unfold before their very own

lives. Misery and anguish because of what the storm put them through and what had to be done to calm the raging storm. However, in order to understand the full context of this story, you must dive a little deeper. Please ensure that you have your diving gear ready and enough oxygen in your tanks.

Let's be clear, no one is asking you to ask someone to spiritually toss you into the deep waters and stormy winds of your raging storm. You are not going to be tossed overboard. It has already been established that you are not in disobedience or fleeing from the presence of the Lord. You have searched your heart in an honest and fair manner, placing yourself in the balance. Yet, you still see no reason for the storm. You have asked God to provide you with an answer. You have reached a state of desperate disposition to obey.

Please bear with me as I conclude this writing, hoping that you will see or learn it the way it was taught to me by the Holy Spirit. I had been exactly where you are, asking the same question, struggling to survive, pushing and shoving, getting nowhere with nothing changing. The storm raged on day after day, week after week, month after month, year after year. The cargo was tossed overboard. The ship was about to break. The mast was broken. Rowing back to shore like a maniac in a bad dream did not work either. Drastic measures were taken with nothing changing. The same drastic measures that you are undertaking will not get you to your destination. Trust me, I tried them.

Time and time again you have been asked to examine your spiritual life for acts of deliberate disobedience and acts of unknown omission. So please, do not feel offended. It is not the intent of this book to make you feel guilty for past acts; acts that have already been forgiven and forgotten. Keep in mind also that this inner search is nothing compared to the three times Peter was asked by the

Lord "Simon, son of Jonah, do you Love me?" (John 21:15-18).

What the Lord is asking you to do is a difficult task that will require you to spiritually prepare yourself for measures that will mark your life forever just like the mariners were affected for life. The Lord is asking you to analyze the story of Jonah from a different point of view, a different perspective. He is asking you to see the events unfolding from the viewpoint of that of the captain and mariners.

To simplify matters, the ship that was entered into by Jonah represents your life. The mariners in your ship is your family and your loved ones. The cargo on board are the blessings and spiritual gifts given to you throughout your Christian living. Most importantly, the captain of the ship heading to Tarshish is you. What about Jonah? Jonah is someone whom you have allowed to board your ship. Jonah is someone who has gone down to the bowels of the ship and has made himself or her-self comfortable while you lose all of your precious cargo. This Jonah has made it into the bowels of your ship unnoticed and fell asleep because you have allowed it to be so.

The bowels of the ship is where activity that keeps the ship moving forward occurs. From food preparation, to propulsion mechanisms, this is where it all happens. Think of a cruise ship. It is in the bowels of the ship where all things happen in order to give you a formidable and unforgettable traveling experience. Likewise in the bowels of your life is where you keep your most inner secrets, emotions, plans for the future, and ideas. It is what propels you. It is where things that manifest pub-licly originate. It implies a personal space and you have allowed it to be violated. How this individual was able to board your ship or come into your life and reach the bowels of your ship may seem incon-sequential now that the storm is in full force. However, the answers to these unknowns must be revealed in order to prevent the same scenario to develop again in the future. What matters now is that he or she is onboard your ship and something must be done with this disobedient individual to rectify the situation and calm the storm.

Your life and the lives of your family, including the blessings that you have obtained by the grace of God, are about to be lost at sea, if you have not lost them already, because you have allowed someone, in an act of kindness, to board your ship. You pray and cry out to the Lord to no avail just like the mariners at sea cried out to their gods. You try to row back to port to no avail. The reason why the storm persists and grows stronger in your life is because you have to go deep into the bowel of your ship and in your prayer closet FIND THE SLEEPER.

You negated to ask your passengers during boarding time some rather important and pertinent questions such as: "What is your occupation? And Where do you come from? What is your country? And of what people are you?'" (Jonah 1:8). In doing so, not asking the questions, you opened yourself to a storm that is overtaking you. Had you ask the proper questions during boarding time, you would not have found yourself asking now; Why Lord? Why Me? Or as the mariners more eloquently asked, "Please (do) tell us (Oh, Lord)! For whose cause is this trouble upon us?

There is no need to cast lots as the times of old. All you need to do is to go into your prayer closet and ask God to grant you the wisdom and discernment to find the sleeper in your ship before it is too late. You have to search for clues that can potentially identify a sleeper in your life and I am ready to help you get started.

Here are some of the clues that I found to be possible indications that there could be a Jonah sleeping in your ship, which proved to be true in my case. Anyone who does not suffer with you during your time of need is an intruder. Anyone who just turns around and tells you that they will be praying for you and continue on their merry way while your ship is taking on water, not losing sleep over your storm is another intruder. Anyone just walking or standing around the deck doing nothing while the storm rages on your life? Bingo! All hands on deck. Anyone willing to toss your cargo overboard while protecting his or hers? Exactly! Have you found anyone actually sleeping? Do any of these scenarios ring a bell? Have you started making a list yet?

You are the captain of your life. You determine who enters your inner circle and who does not. You determine who goes and who stays. You must ask questions. Do not be afraid to ask them. It might make you look suspicious, but so be it. It is your family, your life, your blessings, and your decision to allow, or most importantly, not allow whomever you want to board your ship.

Once you have been led by the Holy Spirit to identify such individuals, as there may be more than one in your life, you must have the courage to toss that person overboard figuratively speaking. That means, no more special treatment or intimate friendship. You are tired of attempting to bring the ship back to shore to no avail. Enough is enough.

You have made it clear that you do not want innocent blood on your hands as you have made every effort to prevent having to throw this intruder into the deep ocean waters. Every row made back to shore cried out for forgiveness. However, you have unknowingly sacrificed enough due to this person's act of disobedience.

Now you understand why you find yourself in the predicament that you are in. You must put an end to it. It is time to calm the storm. Otherwise, you are knowingly risking your life and the lives of your family, your loved ones. You are willingly risking your future blessings. You might not make it to your destination continuing to do what you are currently doing. If you make it, it is by the grace of God, but there will be a high cost associated with it. The cargo will be lost. Loved ones will have perished. Will it be worthy? The decision is yours and yours alone to make.

The hardest part of it all is when the Jonah found in your ship turns out to be your relative or a close friend. You need to be ready to cut ties with everyone for His cause, especially if they are found sleeping through a storm that you believed to be yours but it is actually theirs. You just happened to be caught in it because of the failure to ask the questions proposed by the mariners at sea.

In the Scripture (Matthew 14:22-33) there is a story of the disciples battling a raging storm when Jesus appears to them walking on water. Believing it was a ghost, Peter in his impulsive self yells to

Jesus, "Jesus, if it is you, command me to come to you on the water," (Matthew 14:28) and he steps out of the boat and walks on water. Soon thereafter, he begins to sink, prompting Peter to ask Jesus to help him, to bail him out, saying "Lord, save me!" (Matthew 14:29).

How many times have you stepped out of the boat asking Jesus to help you while you begin to sink? Crying out "Lord, save me.? He rescues you and places you back on the ship, while the storm rages on. These actions have become so repetitive in your life that it is actually getting old, which brings us to this revelation. It is not you who needs to step out of the boat for the storm to subside. It is that disobedient friend or relative who needs to go out into the water.

This intruder will need some motivation to go out there in the storm and get in the waters, face the music. Grab him or her, figuratively speaking, by the back of their shirt/blouse and pants/skirts and toss him/her already. However, before you do so, ask your Jonah to pray to his or her God. Maybe God will have mercy on you. Give your Jonah an opportunity to make things right. If unwilling to pray or repent, then pray as the mariners did; "We pray O Lord, please do not let us perish for this man's life, and do not charge us with innocent blood; for you, O Lord, have done as it pleased you" (Jonah 1: 14) and then, SPLASH.

Doing exactly that which the Holy Spirit leads you to do will cause the storm in your life to dissipate and the tempestuous winds to cease. You will be able to continue on your journey safe from harm, you and your family. It is not an easy task but I assure you that it can be done.

After going down to the bowels of my own ship I was able to identify multiple Jonah type characters. The decision to cut ties was difficult as my Jonahs were close relatives. However, once the decision to 'toss' them overboard was taken, the winds began to change and the waves calmed down, leading to smooth sailings, arriving to the intended destination. Do not worry as to what will be of the Jonahs, the sleepers, for the Lord will prepare a great sea creature that will swallow them and spit them back on land so that they too can be saved.

As a result of my obedience to search and find the sleeper in my life, I have been blessed with a Doctoral degree in Pharmacy, an MBA in Healthcare Management, and now book author. More blessings are yet to come. All for the glory of the Living God. All after tossing my Jonahs overboard.

What will your accomplishments be once your sleeper is found and removed from your inner circle? What sort of blessing will be waiting for you on the other side once the storm subsides? The promotion you seek might come once the sleeper is no longer on your ship. The job you have been praying for might materialize once the sleeper is no longer in your close circle. The education you need for that career change you have been dreaming about might be within reach. Your wife or husband that you have been praying for and waiting for so long may suddenly be introduced in your life once the sleeper or sleepers have been identified and re-moved. Who knows what lies ahead for you, and most importantly, your family and your children. The decision to move forward is yours and yours alone. Remember, the stakes are too high.

However, this story does not only apply to our personal life but also transcends other spaces as well. Organizations in financial storms, including bankruptcy due to loss of customers and sales. Governments in health crisis, including pandemics and deaths. Who you partner with in business makes a difference. A business partner may have offered you a highest price for your goods and ser-vices, but are they interested in seeing you succeed along side of them or are they really after your intellectual property. Could they be working behind your back to destroy you?

Therefore, if you are planning to start a business, ask pertinent questions. In doing so, you will give yourself and your business a better chance to succeed.

Before decisions are made, prayers need to be elevated for wisdom and questions need to be answered. NEVER forget the story of Jonah. Boarding the ship, undetected, Jonah's presence led to a great loss for the captain.

You choose which situation in life you want to find yourself in. The disciples at sea, facing a storm, feared for their lives while Jesus slept. When they could no longer maintain control of the ship they approached Jesus and woke him up from his sleep and asked Him to save them. After scolding his disciples, Jesus then proceeds to rebuke the winds and the waves (Matthew 8:23-27). Similarly, the mariners at sea were facing a storm, fearing for their lives. All while Jonah slept. When all efforts had failed they found Jonah sleeping and asked him to arise and pray. Who would you rather have; Jonah, someone who can stir a storm in your life, or Jesus, the one who can calm the storm in your life? The answer is amazingly and profoundly clear.

I pray for these words to reach your heart and cause you to reflect on your personal and spiritual life, leading to a closer relationship with our Lord and Savior as you seek for a Jonah in the bowels of your ship. May the Lord give you the strength and courage to accept the challenge to . . .

FIND THE SLEEPER

ABOUT THE AUTHOR

Dr. JK Ortiz

Dr. Javier Ortiz is a former Youth Pastor in Orlando FL who has dedicated his life to service. Javier won a poetry writing competition held in Puerto Rico at the age of 14 where he met Abelardo Diaz Alfaro, a world renowned Puerto Rican author. Since, Javier has composed short stories and poems, including songs Porque Te Abates and Quiero Ser Diferente for the Christian Spanish group Cantares.